Rookie
Read-About Science®

All the Colors of the Rainbow

By Allan Fowler

Consultants

Linda Cornwell, Learning Resource Consultant,
Indiana Department of Education

Peter Goodwin, Science Teacher,
Kent School, Kent, Connecticut

Sharyn Fenwick, Elementary Science/Math Specialist
Gustavus Adolphus College, St. Peter, Minnesota

Children's Press®
A Division of Grolier Publishing
New York   London   Hong Kong   Sydney
Danbury, Connecticut

Visit Children's Press® on the Internet at:
http://publishing.grolier.com

Designer: Herman Adler Design Group
Photo Researcher: Caroline Anderson

Library of Congress Cataloging-in-Publication Data

Fowler, Allan.
    All the colors of the rainbow / by Allan Fowler.
        p. cm. — (Rookie read-about science)
    Includes index.
    Summary: Explains how rainbows are formed by the colors in sunlight
shining through water.
    ISBN 0-516-20801-2 (lib. bdg.)   0-516-26415-X (pbk.)
    1. Rainbow—Juvenile literature. 2. Colors—Juvenile literature.
[1. Rainbow.] I. Title. II. Series.
QC976.R2F69   1998   97-28657
551.56'7–dc21   CIP
                                                                              AC

Have you ever seen
a rainbow in the sky?
Its colors are so pretty,
and its shape is so perfect.

You can't touch or grab
hold of a rainbow.

That's because it's made
of sunlight.

Have you ever seen
streams of sunlight
shining in a forest?
They look white.

If sunlight is white, how can it sometimes shine with all the colors of the rainbow?

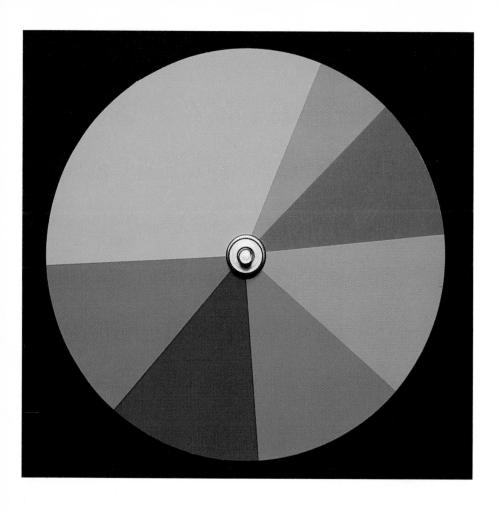

Look at a color wheel. You
can see wedges of colors.

If you spin the wheel gently,
the colors will start to blur.

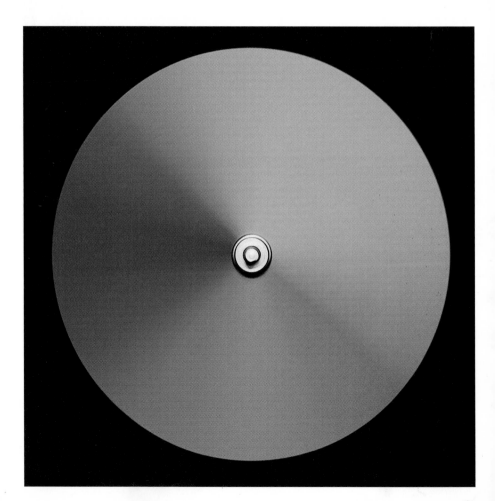

If the wheel spins faster, you will see only white. The blue and yellow and red are still there—you just can't see them.

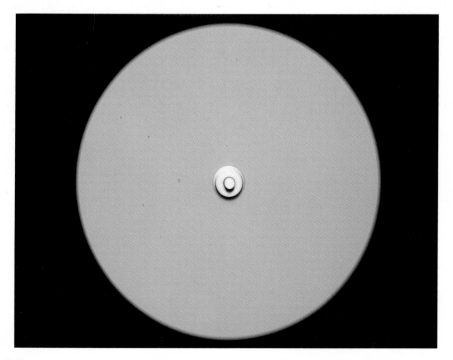

Those same colors are
mixed together in sunlight.

The colors in sunlight are there all the time, but you can only see them once in a while. You might see them if the sun is behind you, and it is raining somewhere in front of you.

When the sunlight enters the raindrops in front of you, the light bounces around and bends inside the water drop.

The light leaves the water drops as separate rays of colored light, which form a rainbow.

You can also see a rainbow's colors when sunlight passes through a specially shaped piece of glass called a prism.

A scientist named Sir Isaac Newton was the first person to explain how a prism works. Like a raindrop, a prism bends sunlight, so you can see all of the different colors.

The color red is always at the top of the rainbow. After that come the colors orange, yellow, green, blue, indigo, and violet. Violet is at the bottom of every rainbow.

When you look at a
rainbow in the sky, you
might not be able to see
all these colors. That's
because they blend together.

Mixing light is similar to
mixing paint. If you mix red
and yellow, you get orange.

So orange lies between red and yellow in a rainbow.

If you mix yellow and blue, you get green.

That's why green lies
between yellow and blue
in a rainbow. Each color
in a rainbow gently blends
into the next color.

Sometimes you can
see two rainbows.

The second one is outside
the first, and not as bright.

Its colors are "upside down,"
with red at the bottom.

The best time to look for
a rainbow is right after
a rainstorm, late in the
afternoon or early in
the morning.

The sun should be low
in the sky.

Stand with your back to
the sun.

If you're lucky, a rainbow
will be right in front
of you.

When you look at a
rainbow from the ground,
it usually looks like a half
of a circle.

But if something blocks the light, you may only see part of the arc.

Not all rainbows are caused by rain. Look for them wherever there is a fine mist of water in the air. You might see a rainbow in a waterfall . . .

. . . or a fountain in a park or even in the spray from a garden hose in your own backyard.

Words You Know

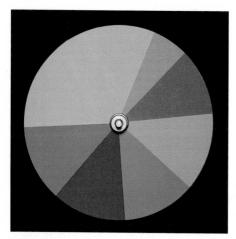

color wheel

prism

rainbow

Sir Isaac Newton

How to look for a rainbow

Index

About the Author

Allan Fowler is a freelance writer with a background in advertising. Born in New York, he lives in Chicago now and enjoys traveling.

Photo Credits